THE RISE AND FALL OF EMPIRES

THE RISE AND FALL OF THE OTTOMAN EMPIRE

DON RAUF

ROSEN PUBLISHING
NEW YORK

Published in 2017 by The Rosen Publishing Group, Inc.
29 East 21st Street, New York, NY 10010

First Edition

Library of Congress Cataloging-in-Publication Data

Names: Rauf, Don, author.
Title: The rise and fall of the Ottoman Empire / Don Rauf.
Description: First edition. | New York : Rosen Publishing, 2017. | Series: The rise and fall of empires | Includes bibliographical references and index. | Audience: Grade 7 to 12.
Identifiers: LCCN 2015049239| ISBN 9781499463446 (library bound) | ISBN 9781499463422 (pbk.) | ISBN 9781499463439 (6-pack)
Subjects: LCSH: Turkey—History—Ottoman Empire, 1288-1918.
Classification: LCC DR485 .R38 2016 | DDC 956/.015—dc23
LC record available at http://lccn.loc.gov/2015049239

Manufactured in China

Contents

INTRODUCTION

Ruling for more than six hundred years, from 1299 until 1922, the Ottoman Empire was one of the biggest and longest-lasting empires in history. At its peak, it spanned from southern Europe and Africa through the Middle East and on to western Asia. This vast realm initially began as disconnected nomadic Turkish tribes. In time,

At its height of power, the Ottoman Empire (sometimes called the Turkish Empire) included parts of southern Europe, northern Africa, and the Arabian Peninsula.

however, these people came together under one great leader, Osman I, to form the beginnings of an organized culture that would grow to become a world power.

The Ottomans would control many cross-continental trade routes. Although united by Islam, the Ottomans respected other religions and encouraged loyalty from other faith groups. In 1453, they would topple the last of the Byzantine Empire when they conquered its capital, Constantinople. Under the rule of Süleyman the Magnificent (who reigned from 1520 to 1566), the empire would reach its peak in terms of the arts, trade, government, unity, and multiculturalism. By recognizing minority groups and supporting their rights, while ruling with absolute control, the Ottomans developed a thriving nation.

Weak leadership, a sickly economy, and wars with neighboring Russia and other countries eventually led to the empire's decline. On the losing side at the end of World War I, the Ottoman Empire was replaced by the Turkish Republic, which continues to this day. The Ottomans left a legacy that included spreading and sustaining the Islamic religion. They also left behind a culture rich in ornate craftsmanship, which can be seen in their carpet weaving, pottery, and architecture. The Ottomans' most visible contribution might be one you see every day (especially if you live near a Starbucks): the coffeehouse.

Chapter 1

A Nation Born from Nomads

The people who eventually formed the Ottoman Empire could trace their roots back to Turkish nomads who traveled from place to place, always in search of better pastures for their livestock. These tribes began in north and northwestern China (Xinjiang) and Mongolia and the eastern part of central Asia. They lived in large expanses of open grasslands called the steppes, which extend all the way west to present-day Hungary. These lands provided food for their sheep, goats, horses, and camels. The grasslands were too dry to raise crops, so the nomads lived as herders. Because of their continuing need to move to a new location, they became skilled horsemen. They also grew to be great fighters, known for their speed and expert marksmanship with the bow and arrow.

To provide themselves with protection from harsh weather, they lived in portable tent-like structures called yurts. They would trade their animals or skins and furs for other products that they needed, such as grains or wood from agricultural communities. Sometimes they would simply raid villages and take supplies they needed.

As early as the sixth century, Chinese texts identified the Turkish nomads who would become the Ottomans. The Chinese gave these people the name *Tujue*. These nomadic people would gradually come together to establish a tribal kingdom Tu-Küe along the Orkhon River in Mongolia and south of Lake Baikal, which is the world's oldest and deepest freshwater lake. These tribes formed political entities called *khanates* that were headed by chiefs called *khans*. They lived under the authority of the Chinese Tang dynasty.

Starting in the 500s, khanates (such as the Uyghurs) came to control a portion of the trade routes known as the Silk Road, which extended all the way west to the Roman Empire. The Silk Road might be described as the first international commercial highway. Merchants transported silk, spices, and other commodities from China to Rome along these routes. Silk (made from silkworms) was especially valued in Rome. It was a fabric Romans did not know how to make and found much more comfortable and luxurious than other fabrics. The Turkish tribes found their power growing as they controlled the Silk Road, and they developed an appreciation for the value of the trade, which would continue in the Ottoman Empire.

THE INFLUENCE OF ISLAM

In 570, at the same time that these early Turkish tribes were rising in power, the prophet Muhammad was born

Islam was the official religion of the Ottoman Empire. These pages from the Qur'an, the religious text of Islam, are written in Arabic calligraphy from the 14th century.

in Mecca, which is now located in Saudi Arabia. According to religious history, Muhammad had a visitation from the angel Gabriel in 610, and over the next twenty-two years, the angel revealed the words of the Qur'an to him. The Qur'an is the holy book of the Islamic religion.

Muhammad and his followers spread the Islamic religion throughout the Arabian Peninsula. After Muhammad died in 632, his followers continued to disseminate his teachings for the next several hundred years through military expeditions, trade, and commerce. Shortly after Muhammad's death, Muhammad's supporters were divided over who should succeed the Prophet. A group called the Sunni believed that Islamic leadership should go to the person in the community deemed best to lead by the Muslim community. For the Sunni, the chain of leadership began with Muhammad's closest companion and then was passed to the "rightly guided" elite who became the first four caliphs (persons considered political and religious successors to the prophet Muhammad).

Another group called the Shia believed that leadership should remain directly within the family line of Muhammad. These views of Islam are at the heart of the Sunni and Shia split that still exists in modern times. Today about 85 to 90 percent of Muslims are Sunni, and 10 to 15 percent are Shia.

Before the Turkish people encountered Islam, they followed different religions. Early on, they worshiped many gods and nature spirits. Holy men called shamans communicated with these gods and spirits. Some early Turks believed in a heaven and a god that could give them luck and power. In the 700s, a Turkish people called the Uyghurs followed many different religions, including shamanism, Buddhism, and Christianity. In the 900s, the Islamic religion had reached the Uyghurs, and most converted. (Today, the Uyghur people number more than eight million and survive as a Muslim group in China. Their connection to modern Turks in the west can be heard in their Turkic language, which is very close to Turkish.)

HORSEMEN AND SLAVE-WARRIORS

The early Turkish military force relied on *gazis* and *mamluks*. The gazis were expert horsemen trained to fight with bows and arrows. These warriors of the Islamic faith often collected taxes and patrolled trade routes for the ruling Turkish tribes, but they also had an independent streak in their nature. They would make their own raids, plundering villages, farms, and cities for what valuables they could find. The mamluks were a military force that started under the Abbasid caliphs. Mamluks were young non-Muslim boys who were captured and brought up to be soldiers. Muhammad, however, taught that slaves were to be regarded as human beings with dignity and rights and not just as property. Mamluks could become a greater part of a society than in other cultures, and they could achieve power and earn incomes.

THE SELJUQ TURKS RIDE TO POWER

Turkish nomadic tribes continued to branch out from the East to the West where they met Muslims who converted them to Islam. In the 900s, the Oghuz Turkish tribe formed in Transoxiana (today's Uzbekistan, Tajikistan, southern Kyrgyzstan, and southwest Kazakhstan). They accepted Islam and became Sunni Muslims. At this time, the Abbasid dynasty based out of Baghdad in today's Iraq (then part of the Islamic empire in much of the Middle East and parts of northern Africa) were the ruling spiritual leaders of Islam in the land. In the eleventh century, one group of Oghuz called the Seljuqs respected the Abbasid religious leader (caliph), but they also wanted to become masters of the land. In pursuit of this control, the Seljuqs slowly built the first truly great Turkish empire. This great Seljuq dynasty would pave way for the Ottoman Empire.

In the mid-eleventh century, Seljuq leader Toghril Beg (also known as Tughril or Togrul) led his *gazis* (horsemen) and *mamluks* (slave-soldiers) into Baghdad. Tughril showed great respect to the Abbasid caliph (kissing the ground before him), but ultimately he forced the Islamic spiritual leader to recognize him as sultan—the new supreme military and political leader of Persia and Mesopotamia. Tughril took control of the caliphate's armies and eliminated Arabs from government. While the caliph maintained spiritual authority over the empire, Tughril and the Seljuq sultanate controlled all other aspects of the empire. The Seljuqs, who were Sunni, grew in power and took over territories in the Middle East. This rise of the Seljuqs is one of the reasons that much of the region remains Sunni to this day.

A PUSH INTO BYZANTINE LANDS

After Tughril died in 1063, his nephew Alp-Arslan (the "Lion Hero") assumed power and expanded territories farther west. His armies invaded the land mass known as Anatolia, also called Asia Minor. Today Anatolia makes up most of modern-day Turkey, which is bordered by the Black Sea to the north and the Mediterranean Sea to the south.

During the time of Alp-Arslan's rule, the Byzantine or Eastern Roman Empire controlled much of eastern Anatolia, but the "Lion Hero" was determined to conquer it.

The Byzantine Empire rose to power under the reign of Constantine the Great. In the year 330, Emperor Constantine founded the capital of Eastern Roman Christian Empire in Byzantium, a former ancient Greek city. He renamed the city Constantinople, which later became Istanbul under the Ottoman Empire. The great city was situated in a prized location—just east of the Bosporus Strait, the channel of water that separates Europe from Asia. This channel is important because it connects the Black Sea to the Sea

Alp-Arslan *(left)*, sultan of the Seljuq Turks, whose name means "Lion Hero," defeated the Byzantine army and took the emperor Romanus IV Diogenes *(right)* as prisoner in 1071.

of Marmara. The Marmara then connects to the Aegean Sea via the Dardanelles Strait. Constantinople became a trading hub—a critical point between Europe in the West and Asia in the East. The city attracted large numbers of foreigners who came to buy and sell goods in its market.

Although the Western Roman Empire collapsed in 476 under attacks by barbarians led by the German warrior Odoacer, the Byzantine Empire—with its strong government operations, political stability, and relative wealth—survived for hundreds of years to come before heading into decline.

In 1071, Alp-Arslan and his soldiers were weakening the Byzantine Empire, taking its cities in eastern Anatolia. A turning point came when Alp-Arslan and his Seljuq tribe took the major city of Manzikert. After a fierce battle, the Byzantine emperor Romanos IV Diogenes and his men surrendered. Upon meeting Romanos, Alp-Arslan placed his boot on the emperor's throat and forced him to kiss the ground. The defeat marked a major shift in power as the Turks controlled more of Anatolia. John Doukas, the next ruler of Byzantium, ordered the disgraced Romanos to be blinded.

THE SELJUQ EMPIRE RULES

The Seljuqs then entered a period of uneasy peace with the Byzantine Empire, while gaining a foothold in Anatolia. Over the next ten years, the Seljuqs would push steadily westward, gaining control of most of this land. Muslim Turkish officials replaced the former Byzantine leaders throughout the countryside. The Islamic religion and Turkish customs and language spread. Seljuq rule lasted in Anatolia for 230 years starting in 1077. The region became the Sultanate of Rum (Rum meaning Rome, representing the region's former status as part of the Eastern Roman Empire).

In 1095, the emperor of Byzantium, Alexius I Comnenus, sent representatives to the pope in Italy to ask for help against the Turks. With Christian forces from the pope, the Byzantines regained the western third of Anatolia.

Despite these losses, the Seljuqs of Rum would control a major portion of Anatolia throughout the 1100s and 1200s and capture key Byzantine port cities along the Mediterranean and Black seas. The Sultanate of Rum is said to have reached its peak from 1220 to 1237 under sultan Allaeddin Keykubad.

Seljuq sultan Allaeddin Keykubad commissioned the Yivli Minare, seen here, which is one of the oldest Seljuq monuments in Antalya, Turkey. Minarets are tall towers from which Islamic holy men call Muslims to prayer.

Under his rule, trade increased, and mosques, *medreses* (schools), hospitals, palaces, and bridges were built. However, struggles for leadership and the independent nature of Turkish tribes contributed to disunity and an inability to maintain a centralized government.

A MONGOL THREAT

A year after Keykubad's death in 1237, the Mongols, a fierce nomadic people from central Asia, began to overrun the Sultanate of Rum, leading to its downfall. In 1243, after the Mongols defeated the Seljuqs in battle in northeast Anatolia, central and eastern Anatolia became a Mongol protectorate. Rum survived in name only until into the fourteenth century—dwindling and then disappearing completely.

In 1260, the Mongols were looking to expand their influence as far as they could. More than three decades after the death of their most famous leader, Genghis Khan, the Mongols swept through the Middle East—including present-day Iran, Iraq, and Syria. Hulegu Khan, a grandson of Genghis Khan, led the Mongol armies. When Hulegu pushed on into Egypt, the Mamluks of Egypt stopped his furious charge. They defeated the advancing Mongols at a decisive fight in Ain Jalut in Palestine. This battle was one of the earliest in which firearms were said to have been used. The Mamluks used weapons called hand cannons that were primitive but may have helped frighten off the Mongols. In 1277, the Mamluks attacked the Mongols in the Sultanate of Rum, disrupting their power in Anatolia.

Chapter 2

THE RISE OF THE OTTOMANS

With the Seljuq tribes now weakened, the Ottomans rose to power. Led by a man named Osman (born in 1258), the Turks who lived in northwest Anatolia were coming together and gaining strength. (They were called Ottomans, a corruption of Osman's name, originally known in English as Othman.) Legend has it that Osman once had a dream in which a tree grew out of his chest. Its roots and branches grew to cover Asia, Europe, and Africa. The dream was prophetic—a harbinger of the vast Ottoman Empire to come.

Osman I (1258–1324) was the founder of the Ottoman Empire. Under his rule, the Turkish people and Muslim warriors called gazis captured many towns from the Byzantines.

Starting in 1299, Osman led his state (called a *beylik*),

which bordered the remaining Byzantine Empire. It was centered around the town of Sogut. Osman was known as a man of the people, and he brought together many tribes. As a brilliant rider and swordsman himself, Osman I gained the respect of the gazi horsemen. Nomadic Turkish tribes still fleeing the Mongol hordes in the East came to Osman's beylik and gave him their support.

During the first few decades of the 1300s, Osman and his soldiers successfully fought the Byzantines, capturing territories north, west, and south of Sogut. As this new Ottoman domain grew, Osman established tax-collecting among its citizens to support the new kingdom. In the year of Osman's death, 1326, the Ottomans finally seized the major walled Byzantine city of Bursa. The siege had lasted an estimated six to nine years.

Making Bursa the Ottoman capital, Osman's son Orhan, with his striking blond beard, assumed power, and the Ottoman advance gained speed. After the cities of Nicaea, Nicomedia, and Scutari fell in quick succession, the Ottomans took command of lands closer to Constantinople. From the walls of the Byzantine capital, citizens could now see the fledgling Ottoman Empire.

A SIGNIFICANT STEP INTO EUROPE

For the Byzantine Empire and Constantinople to survive even in its smaller, weakened form, Byzantine emperor John VI Cantacuzene negotiated with the sultan Orhan. He married off his daughter Theodora to Orhan in 1346 and promised them certain Byzantine lands. In the 1340s, the

Byzantine Empire was also at war with invading Serbs, and in 1349, the Serbs had seized Salonica, the Byzantine Empire's second largest city. With the help of Orhan's son, the general Süleyman, and twenty thousand Ottoman warriors, Salonica was recaptured for the Byzantine Empire. (In 1387, however, the Ottomans would have a change of heart and take Salonica for themselves.)

In return for the help, Cantacuzene allowed the Ottomans to cross the Dardanelles channel. The Ottomans were now in Europe. In 1354, they conquered the Byzantine city of Gallipoli, which became their first permanent European base and, later, the site of a costly battle in World War I. Now firmly situated in Europe, the Turks swiftly went on to conquer cities throughout Thrace (which today is northeastern Greece), the European part of Turkey, and southeastern Bulgaria in the Balkan Peninsula.

After Orhan died in 1360, power transferred to his son, Murat I. Murat I expanded into Europe, taking the major Byzantine city of Adrianople in 1361. He made it the new capital of the Ottoman Empire, renaming it Edirne. With Edirne as a base, the Ottomans continue to advance, taking more of Bulgaria and parts of Greece.

Still, the ultimate prize—Constantinople—was not theirs. The city was heavily fortified, protected by immense walls, which the Ottomans knew would be almost impossible to penetrate. In 1363, the ever-shrinking Byzantium signed a treaty with Murat I, confirming all the Ottoman conquests in Europe and promising not to conspire against them. In return, Murat would not attack the city and would provide it with needed food.

DEVSIRME AND THE JANISSARIES

One of Murat's lasting but complicated legacies was the creation of elite infantry units called *janissaries* in 1376. The word comes from the Turkish *yeniçeri* (*yeni* meaning new, and *ceri* meaning soldier). The janissaries were paid troops loyal only to the sultan. Similar to the mamluks, janissary forces were manned by Christian boys who were captured by the Ottomans and put into service. This practice was called *devsirme*. It was like a human tax imposed on captured Christian communities. The enslaved boys were taught Turkish and given the best military training, and they converted to Islam. They became an effective, almost unstoppable fighting machine. In return, they received respect in the community, a cash salary, and confiscated riches. In time, however, they grew to become more independent, making demands and questioning the sultan. In 1826, Sultan Mahmud abolished the janissaries after they revolted. Mahmud formed regular drilled troops of Muslims. When the janissaries refused to give up power, Mahmud sent troops to capture them. His soldiers killed about seven thousand janissaries while fifteen thousand or so were sent into exile.

The janissaries were an elite military force. Janissary recruits were Christian boys who were enslaved to serve the Ottoman sultan and converted to Islam.

CONTROLLING THE VASSAL STATES

The Ottomans were often able to retain power in so many areas by having the regional leaders swear allegiance to the Ottoman Empire. In return for this allegiance, the Ottomans allowed regional rulers to keep their titles and some local power. They became "vassal" states, meaning they were granted use of the land but were subordinate to the empire. Vassal states maintained some autonomy, but any uprising would be firmly put down.

Serbia became a vassal to the Ottomans in 1387, but by 1388, the Serbian princes had grown unhappy with the situation. They formed a pact with Bulgarian warlords and Bosnian allies, and banding together, they drove the Ottomans out of Bosnia. Looking to stop this rebellion, the Turks returned to do battle in 1389.

On June 15 of that year, the Serbs, led by Prince Lazar, and the Ottomans, led by Murat, clashed in a costly fight at Kosovo Field ("the field of blackbirds") involving tens of thousands of soldiers. At the battle, a Serbian nobleman faked his surrender and stabbed Murat to death. Murat's son Beyazit captured Prince Lazar and had him beheaded. The bulk of both armies were killed, but in the end the Ottomans prevailed, proving that they could achieve a major battle victory on European soil. After the battle, Serbian principalities fell in line as Ottoman vassals.

With the death of his father, Beyazit took the throne and promptly had his brother Yidrum murdered to get rid of any challenge to his claim as sultan. Because of his skill at lightning-fast attacks, Beyazit gained the nickname "Thunderbolt." Two years after becoming sultan, Beyazit launched major campaigns into Albania, Macedonia, and Greece. In July 1393, he captured Tarnovo, the capital of Bulgaria, and from that point, Bulgaria remained under Turkish rule for five hundred years.

Nicknamed Thunderbolt, the Ottoman sultan Beyazit was known for his fast military strikes, including one at the western city of Nicopolis in Greece, pictured here.

CRUSADERS AND MONGOLS DESCEND AGAIN

Beyazit was determined to take Constantinople and put the city under siege starting in 1393, but the spread of his Muslim empire was causing concerns in Christian Europe. King Sigismund of Hungary organized a crusade against the Ottomans. In 1396, he led a Christian army of one hundred thousand down the Danube to northwestern Greece. Responding with a force of two hundred thousand men, Beyazit handily obliterated the crusaders, and Sigismund barely escaped. Beyazit turned his attentions back to Constantinople but abandoned his attacks in 1399 when a new threat approached from the East.

At this time, Mongols were gaining power and territory under a warlord king who walked with a limp because half of his body was paralyzed. This Mongol leader was known as Timur or Tamerlane. Despite his handicap, he was one of the most brutal warriors of all time. He would bury his enemies alive, cement them into walls, slice them in two at the waist, trample them to death with horses, or behead them. In 1402, Beyazit led his armies to battle Timur in Ankara in present-day Turkey. Beyazit was depending on loyalties of tribal chiefs in that region, but Timur had built new relationships with them, and they abandoned Beyazit. The Ottomans suffered a major loss. Timur captured Beyazit, and as the story goes, he kept the sultan in a cage until he died a year later. In three more years, the mighty Mongolian Timur would also die after catching cold.

CHAPTER 3

THE EMPIRE STRIKES BACK

The capture and death of Beyazit weakened the Ottomans, and they spent a period of time trying to reorganize and regain strength. Beyazit's sons took over different parts of the realm. When they fought each other for complete control of the kingdom, the youngest, Mehmet, came out the winner in 1413. He spent the next eight years trying to regain control of Anatolia and the Balkans.

When Mehmet's son Murat II came to power at age seventeen, the teenager already had experience in battle. Although he attempted (and failed) to take Constantinople in 1422, he went on to conquer northern Greece in 1430. Just as the Ottomans were determined to expand, the Christian crusaders were determined to stop them. In 1443, King Wladyslaw, ruler of Hungary and Poland, launched another crusade against the Turks. Both sides suffered heavy losses, and in 1444, Wladyslaw and Murat signed a treaty agreeing to a ten-year truce.

At age forty, in September of 1444, Murat II shocked his court when he announced that he would retire as the leader of the Ottoman Empire and turn control over to his twelve-year-old son, Mehmet II. While he had great faith in the boy, court advisers did not, and when an emergency came, Murat II resumed leadership. Mehmet's leadership would have wait, but when his time came, it would lead to the Ottomans' biggest victory of all.

THE CONSTANT CURSE OF CRUSADERS

About a month after King Wladyslaw had agreed to peace, he broke his treaty and was leading a new army of crusaders back into Ottoman Balkan lands. At first, Wladyslaw and his men made great gains against Murat, but Murat

The Ottoman Empire was besieged many times by Christian crusaders. In 1444, the Ottomans fought the Battle of Varna in Bulgaria, defeating the Christian army and killing its leader, King Wladyslaw.

and his janissaries initiated a counterattack that resulted in the death of Wladyslaw. Without their leader, the crusaders became disorganized. They either fled or were killed or enslaved.

After putting down the crusaders, Murat turned his attention to problems within his government. The janissaries were now rebelling, demanding an increase in pay. In protest, they burned down the market in Edirne. Murat gave into their pay demands, an action that validated their power. In time, these elite soldiers would become so strong that the sultans would fear them. For the time being, however, with the janissaries appeased, Murat would go on to seize more land in Greece and Albania.

THE YOUNG CONQUEROR OF CONSTANTINOPLE

After three decades of effectively ruling the empire, Murat had a stroke and died. Now it was Mehmet's time. Just a month away from his nineteenth birthday in 1451, Mehmet II again became sultan of the Ottoman Empire. One of his first orders of business was to have his one-year-old half brother executed to eliminate any threat to his power. He justified the killing saying that fratricide was now part of Ottoman code.

Then Mehmet turned his focus to Constantinople. The walled city was now all that survived of the Byzantine Empire. It had survived twenty-three attacks over one thousand years. Mehmet believed it was his destiny to take the city, fulfilling a prophecy by Muhammad himself.

Two years after becoming sultan, in 1453, Mehmet began a fifty-four-day siege of the city. Inside its walls, defending Constantinople, were only about five thousand soldiers. Outside the walls, Mehmet assembled about eighty thousand to two hundred thousand to attack. He pummeled the city with artillery from about seventy cannons. Mehmet thought the cannon barrage would allow for an easy breach of the walls, but the Byzantine defenders of the city quickly repaired the walls.

Mehmet also wanted to attack Constantinople by sea, but to prevent this type of assault, the Byzantines had stretched a great chain across the Great Horn, the ancient harbor of Constantinople. No chain would block Mehmet. He ordered that a road of oiled tree branches be built over a hill connecting the Bosporus strait to the harbor. Using this track, Mehmet's soldiers hauled warships over land, circumventing the chain, and lowered the battle ships into the Great Horn. The Byzantine emperor Constantine and his army were stunned.

With the conquest of Constantinople on May 29, 1453, the twenty-one-year-old Ottoman Sultan Mehmet II brought an end to the Byzantine Empire, which had lasted 1,123 years.

THE BIG BANG THEORY

In 1452, the final Byzantine emperor, Constantine (who had the same name as the very first Byzantine emperor), saw the impending threat from Mehmet. Constantine consulted with a Hungarian cannon maker named Orban, who offered to build him cannons to protect Constantinople. Because Constantine did not have the money to pay Orban, the cannon maker traveled 140 miles (225 kilometers) west to Edirne to meet with Mehmet. Mehmet agreed to pay Orban to make a cannon large enough to smash the walls at Constantinople. Orban made him a cannon that could shoot a 1,500-pound (680-kilogram) ball. Although it took three hours to reload and collapsed after six weeks, Orban's cannon—one of the largest cannons ever built—was imposing on the battlefield and helped the Ottomans overtake Constantinople.

Before the final battle, Constantine and his people prayed within the magnificent Christian basilica, the Hagia Sophia, which literally means "Holy Wisdom," built by the Roman emperor Justinian in the 500s. On May 29, 1453, the intense bombardment finally made a break in Constantinople's walls through which the Ottoman army entered with Mehmet leading on his white horse. Constantine died with his soldiers in a final fight for the Christian city.

At first, Mehmet allowed his troops to sack the city, but he put a stop to it when he realized the beauty of Constantinople. He wanted to preserve its structures for his use. "What a city we have given over to plunder and destruction," said Mehmet, according to his Greek biographer Kritoboulos.

Mehmet repaired the ancient walls and built many public buildings—hospitals, colleges, and public baths. He built Islamic medreses. He also built Topkapi Palace, which would be home to future sultans and the administrative, educational, and art center of the empire. It was really a city within a city surrounded by a wall three miles (five kilometers) long. The population within the palace itself would reach as many as five thousand, including many janissaries.

A few days after the conquest, Mehmet converted the Hagia Sophia into a mosque. People widely began referring to the city as Istanbul, and it replaced Edirne as the new capital. In converting the city to an Islamic capital, Mehmet built more mosques, as well as a naval shipyard and arsenal.

After Mehmet built Topkapi Palace, overlooking the Sea of Marmara, it became one of the major residences of the sultans, their harems, servants, and soldiers for about four hundred years.

A THRIVING, NEW ISTANBUL

Although Istanbul would be the Muslim capital, Mehmet believed that diversity was crucial to the city's revitalization. He invited Christians and Jews to live there. By 1454, a year after the conquest of Constantinople, Mehmet had institutionalized the "millet system," which "tolerated clients of the Muslim community." Minority religious, ethnic, and geographical communities were given a limited amount of power to regulate their own affairs, but the Ottoman government maintained absolute supremacy. Large numbers of Greeks, Armenians, and Turks repopulated the city, bringing its numbers from just a few thousand to fifty thousand in a few years.

Mehmet saw himself not only as sultan but as the next caesar, ruler of the Roman Empire (although Christian Europe did not recognize his claim). He proclaimed himself as the protector of the Greek Christian church, and he appointed a new patriarch (Christian church leader) of the city. With the conquest of Constantinople, the world officially recognized the Ottoman Empire. Mehmet, who was only twenty-one years old, was now one of the world's most powerful leaders.

Mehmet demonstrated that he was more than just a warrior. He had a strong interest in literature, fine arts, and architecture. He is said to have spoken seven languages. He founded many colleges and universities, some of which are still active. He established criminal and constitutional

Culture and the arts began to flourish throughout the Ottoman Empire in the fifteenth century. A highlight was the production of high quality ceramic wares from the town of Iznik.

law. Under his rule, the Code of Law (*Kanun-name*) was written. It concerned administrative and criminal justice, military affairs, discipline of statesmen, and the organization of the religious hierarchy.

Mehmet also continued to wage several wars to expand the empire, taking territories in Asia Minor, Bosnia, the Kingdom of Serbia, and Albania.

Chapter 4

The Ottomans Reach Their Zenith

When Mehmet died at age forty-nine, his son Beyazit took power. Beyazit firmly established Istanbul as an economically viable city. As he built the central treasury, he reinforced the army, constructed huge warships for the navy, and increased the number of janissaries, equipping them with handguns. Under his leadership, the Turkish sea gazis, or warriors, took on great strength in the Mediterranean Sea, dominating the Venetians of Italy who had controlled the seas.

Like his father, Sultan Beyazit welcomed others. He welcomed Jewish refugees from Spain, who were expelled by the Catholic monarchs Ferdinand and Isabella. Beyazit said that by expelling the Jews, Ferdinand "impoverished his own country and enriched mine!" Beyazit threatened death to all those who treated Jews harshly. He was also known to give to the poor (supporting those in poverty is one of the five pillars of Islam). He enjoyed literature and poetry as well.

In 1512, Selim I became sultan and acquired the nickname "the Grim" after murdering all his male relatives so that he would have no competition for his claim to power.

FROM GIVING TO GRIM

In 1512, Beyazit's son, Selim I gained the support of the janissaries and overthrew his father, who died that year. Selim's rule was a short eight years between 1512 and 1520, but during that time he tripled the size of the Ottoman Empire. The new sultan was nicknamed Selim the Grim because he murdered all his male relatives to make sure he would have sole claim to the throne. He kept the treasury full and compensated the janissaries handsomely.

In 1514, Selim battled the shah, or leader, of Iran who led Shiite Muslims. These Shiites opposed the

Ottoman Sunnis. In a hard-fought battle, Selim and a force of 120,000 troops defeated Shah Ismail and his army of 70,000. Although wounded, Ismail recovered strength and again developed a Shia stronghold in Iran.

In 1517, the Ottomans went to war against the Mamluks of Egypt, acquiring northern Egypt and the entire Islamic Mamluk empire, which included the Islamic holy cities of Mecca and Medina. As the guardian of these holy cities, Selim took on the title of caliph, meaning he was to be considered both political leader and the supreme religious leader of the Muslim community. When Selim I died at age fifty, the Ottoman Empire covered almost one billion acres.

A KINGDOM AT ITS MOST MAGNIFICENT

In 1520, at age twenty-six, Süleyman I succeeded his father, Selim. His forty-six-year rule was the longest of the Ottoman Empire and recognized as the apex of Ottoman achievement. The grandeur of the empire would never be greater. Süleyman would become known as Süleyman the Magnificent.

Süleyman's rule was noted for great prosperity and expansion. Here, the sultan grants Hungarian King John II Sigismund Zapolya permission to resume his throne after Hungary's defeat by the Ottomans.

He was able to balance the demands of the religious establishment with the ambitions of the army. He created and organized laws that complemented the laws of Islam, which are called *sharia*. He was known as *kanuni* (law giver) and established many laws, called *kanuns*, related to society, education, taxation, and crime. The rights and obligations of leaders and citizens were clearly laid out. Süleyman was considered gracious and fair. When he discovered that a tax coming from Egypt was very high, he researched the matter and found that a tyrannical governor there was overcharging the people. Süleyman replaced the governor immediately.

THE WORLD'S TRADE CENTER

Istanbul became a major trading center. The Ottomans conducted trade with Europeans. Controlling many trade routes from the East, the Turks would bring in spices from India as well as silk, musk, Chinese porcelain, and rhubarb (known as a cure for diarrhea, jaundice, and various skin complaints) from the East. From Russia came amber, timber, furs, and grain. From Europe, the Ottomans imported goods that they did not make for themselves: woolen cloth, glassware, and some special manufactured goods like medicine, gunpowder, and clocks. Agricultural goods made up many of the Ottoman exports, typically Mediterranean crops like grapes, figs, and olive oil. Trading points were set up in Aleppo, Damascus, and Cairo. The

Ottomans took many steps to protect traders from attacks and set up *caravanserais*, places where caravans of traders could rest along their routes. The government coffers filled with taxes collected on the trading business.

In 1555, Istanbul was introduced to coffee—roasting the beans, grinding them, and slowly cooking them in hot water. From this discovery, coffeehouse culture was born. In the new capital, a market called the Grand Bazaar grew with a myriad of shops and merchants selling all types of goods.

The Grand Bazaar in Istanbul is one of the oldest and largest covered markets in the world. It was the trade center of commerce under the Ottoman Empire.

Istanbul flourished with the construction of dams, aqueducts, fountains, medreses, baths, bridges, and gardens. Providing for the people was a top concern so hospitals, libraries, orphanages, and kitchens to feed the poor were also built.

The mosques built by Mimar Sinan (a Christian who was captured and put into service under devsirme) were considered the greatest architectural triumphs of the Islamic world. Looking out to the Golden Horn, his Mosque of Süleyman (Süleymaniye), completed in 1558, is considered by many to be his masterpiece. Istanbul was alive with energy as a center for visual art, music, writing, and philosophy.

LIFE IN THE HAREMS

The Ottoman family structure was patriarchal with men leading the families and women working at home, providing food and necessities for the family. Among the Ottoman ruling class and wealthy, men would take on several wives and mistresses who were kept in a dwelling place called the harem. The Qur'an allowed men to legally have four wives and an unlimited number of concubines. The harem did not just exist to serve the men's desires. Mothers would also live there, and children were raised there as well. Depending on the harem, women might be taught about Islam, the Turkish language, reading, calligraphy, and history. Some learned to sing and play music. The mother of the reigning sultan lived in the harem and was called the *valide sultan*. She ruled over the harem and often had influence over the sultan.

The Mosque of Sultan Süleyman is the largest mosque in Istabul and considered to be one of the greatest designs by the celebrated Ottoman architect Mimar Sinan.

Süleyman supported the arts and artisans who perfected calligraphy, miniature painting, tile making, and textile design. Craftsmen took pride in making ornate and intricate creations, found in Turkish bookbinding, woodwork, and tools. The magnificent sultan particularly loved poetry and wrote almost three thousand poems himself under the pen name Muhibbi.

Although Süleyman's reign was highlighted by cultural growth, he also expanded the empire. He conquered Christian centers in Belgrade (the capital of Serbia), Rhodes (Greece), and most of Hungary (killing the king). Transylvania came under his domain. Süleyman installed governors in Algiers, Tunis, and Tripoli in northern Africa. He captured most of the Venetian-held Aegean islands.

Süleyman had only a few failures—notably attempts to take over Vienna in 1529 and Malta in 1565.

CHAPTER 5

THE DECLINE OF THE OTTOMAN EMPIRE

A year after his attempt to take Malta in 1566, Süleyman died, and his son Selim II took power. The reign of Selim II was the turning point of powerful leadership for the Ottomans and the beginning of a long decline. Selim did conquer Crete and Tunis in the 1570s, but the next sixteen sultans were seen as men of little ability, confidence, or experience. Many of these sultans did not lead on the battlefield. Many came to power only knowing the pleasures of palace life. Often their chief adviser, called the grand *vizier*, would actually be in control.

The Ottoman Empire was no longer expanding, and European countries were making expeditions to the "New World" (the Americas), where they were gaining new wealth. Europeans gradually advanced technologically and militarily to surpass the Ottomans. A major milestone in the decline of the empire came in 1683 when Sultan Mehmet IV was convinced that if the Ottomans could take Vienna, then all Christians would obey them. Christian forces, however, repelled the Ottomans' two-month long attack. One legend says that Viennese bakers created the croissant after this victory, shaping it like a crescent seen on the Ottoman flag.

Encouraged by this success, Christian powers in Europe brought together a Holy League consisting of the Holy Roman Empire (based in Austria), the Venetian Republic, and Poland in 1684 to reclaim territory from the Ottomans. In 1686, Russia also joined the fight. These forces freed Hungary from Ottoman control in 1687. A decisive victory by the Austrian army at the Battle of Zenta in Serbia brought an end to Ottoman power in central and southeastern Europe.

Another milestone of decline was the invasion of Egypt by Napoleon Bonaparte of France in 1798. Napoleon made conquests along the coast, and the French maintained a presence there until 1801 when they were forced out by joint British and Ottoman forces. When the French left, Muhammad Ali became the Ottoman sultan's viceroy in Egypt. He became known as the father of modern Egypt, closing the door to Ottoman influence and opening the ways to Egypt's future independence.

The Austrian victory at the Battle of Zenta in September 1697 marked the end of the Ottoman control in central and southeastern Europe.

REFORMS ARE NOT ENOUGH

During his rule from 1789 to 1807, Sultan Selim III made early reforms to Westernize and help keep the Ottoman Empire together so that it remained competitive in a changing world. The empire was falling into social, economic, and administrative chaos, so he put forth a series of new regulations called "the new order," which were intended to modernize the Ottomans. He was battling against bureaucracy, overstaffing, and corruption.

With the help of European advisors, Selim, who was also a poet and composer, opened factories and technical schools. He established Ottoman embassies in London, Vienna, Berlin, and Paris. He studied European practices and introduced a European-style military. He also built new army and naval schools for the systemized training of soldiers. However, rebellion among the janissaries and conservative people of influence pushed him to abandon reform.

From 1821 to 1830, Greece revolted for independence, wanting to be governed under a Greek Orthodox Christian authority rather than Muslim. Around this time, Serbia was also revolting, and Bulgaria, Romania, and Montenegro were making moves toward independence. Russia had an interest in the countries in the Balkans and aided their independence movements. Russia also wanted greater influence in these areas and control of waters around the Black Sea as well as the straits of the Bosporus and Dardanelles in order to improve its trade and economy.

Similar to Selim III, sultans Abdulmecid I and Abdulaziz pushed forward a series of reforms called Tanzimat, meaning "reorganization," from 1839 to 1876. The basis of the reforms were policies that guaranteed security of life, property, liberty, and honor of all subjects regardless of religion or race. These policies were intended to prevent revolt and encourage peoples to stay within the empire. But the great tide toward independence in Ottoman territories was now unstoppable.

THE SICK MAN OF EUROPE

Europe and Russia now recognized that the power of the Ottoman Empire was waning. As early as 1853, Tsar Nicholas of Russia said: "We have on our hands a sick man, a very sick man." Europeans countries and Russia, however, were not in agreement on how to handle this ailing empire.

The "Sick Man of Europe" now tried to develop allegiances with the superpowers to protect itself. In 1851, the Ottomans recognized France and Napoleon III as the supreme Christian authority of the Holy Land, which included much of the Ottomans' European territory. Russia made counter claims that it was the protector of the Christian faith in Ottoman lands. As this rivalry between France and Russia built, Britain also had an interest in opposing Russia and maintaining the Ottoman Empire.

In 1853, Russian troops entered the Ottoman Danube provinces, and Russian warships in the Black Sea destroyed Turkish vessels. Alarmed by the aggressive Russian forces, Britain and France banded together to help the Ottomans in the Crimean War (1853–56). Russia was defeated and forced to destroy its Black Sea fleet. In the Treaty of Paris, the Ottoman Empire regained certain territories and acceptance by European powers as "an equal." Its territorial integrity was guaranteed by Britain and France, but these guarantees were not worth much.

To fight the Crimean War, the Ottomans had borrowed greatly. The empire was shouldering enormous debt and heading closer to economic collapse. Additionally, Russia, stung by the loss of the Crimean War, was developing a foreign policy intent on revenge.

Starting in the 1600s, Russia fought the growing Ottoman Empire. After the Russian victory in the Russo-Turkish War of 1877–78 (pictured), the Ottomans lost much of their European territories.

In the 1870s, a group of Ottoman intellectuals and poets calling themselves the Young Ottomans pushed for a constitutional and parliamentary government. While the sultan kept full overall power, representatives were elected, and a parliament with two houses came together in the spring of 1877. Around that same time, however, Russia launched a new war with the Ottomans (the Russo-Turkish War of 1877–78). The sultan suspended the parliament and constitution to take care of the new crisis.

Russia moved swiftly and had its sights on taking over Istanbul. Again, Britain became concerned, intervened, and moved a fleet to the area. Austria-Hungary, too, was distressed by the Russian advance. The superpowers of the world—England, Russia, Germany, Austria-Hungary, France, and Italy—met in Berlin in 1878 to end the conflict. In the Treaty of Berlin, they agreed that Romania, Serbia, Bosnia-Herzegovina, and Montenegro were to be freed from Ottoman rule. Bulgaria proper became an independent state but with some control over it by the Ottoman sultan. Macedonia remained part of the Ottoman Empire. Russia, in the end, wound up with very little. Although the Ottoman Empire lost a good deal of territory, the European powers guaranteed its "integrity."

The European powers, however, were not going to respect Ottoman boundaries. In 1881, the French conquered Tunisia and made it a protectorate. In 1882, the British took over Egypt. Italy laid claim to lands in Eritrea in northern Africa. More and more of the Ottoman Empire was disappearing.

YOUNG TURKS AND THE ARMENIAN GENOCIDE

In the 1890s, young Armenians were pressing for reforms in the Ottoman Empire. They called for a constitutional government, the right to vote, and an end to discriminatory practices such as taxes levied solely against them because they were Christians. The Ottoman sultan feared this uprising and slaughtered over one hundred thousand Armenian citizens between 1894 and 1896.

In 1895, a reform group called the Young Turks (officially the Committee of Union and Progress) were gaining power, pushing for an elected parliament and a constitution, just as the Young Ottomans had. In 1909, the Young Turks forced the sultan Abdul Hamet II from power, and a constitutional monarchy was established.

Many Turks and Armenians were hopeful for a more just and fair government. The Young Turks promoted industrialization, education for women, and improved primary schools.

In 1913, however, three of the Young Turks seized control of the government and became ruthless dictators in their own way. They became known as the "Three Pashas." They wanted to create a new Turkish empire and unite all Turkic peoples from Turkey's eastern border through to central Asia. They would call this new land Turan, and it would have only one religion—Islam. A large Christian Armenian population, however, was standing in their way. A campaign to kill and deport Armenians began and continued through World War I. It is estimated that 1.5 million Armenians died between 1915 and 1923—an event recognized as genocide by the United Human Rights Council and many nations. To this day, these atrocities have continued to strain Armenian-Turkish relations.

WORLD WAR I BRINGS AN END OF AN ERA

The end of the Ottoman Empire came with World War I. On June 28, 1914, war was sparked when a Serbian terrorist assassinated the archduke Franz Ferdinand, heir to the Austro-Hungarian Empire. Austria-Hungary declared war on Serbia. What seemed like a small conflict quickly spread to become a full world war. When Germany saw Russia move to help Serbia, it declared war on Russia. France and Britain then aligned with Russia, becoming known as the Allied Powers, and Italy and the United States later entered the battle on their side.

The Ottoman Empire sided with the Central Powers (Austria-Hungary and Germany) and joined the battle in 1914. Before the war, Germany and the Ottomans had agreed to build an extensive railway that would connect Berlin to Baghdad. This project gave economic support to the Ottomans, and based on this connection, the Ottomans (headed by the Young Turks) signed a formal alliance with Germany. When war started, Germany pressured the Ottomans to join the fight, threatening to pull its economic and military assistance. The Turks hoped the war would protect them from Russia (its long-time enemy) and help them regain lost territory.

In 1915, the British and French launched an ill-fated attack in the Dardanelles and the peninsula of

With its defeat in World War I, the Ottoman Empire came to an end. Pictured are Turkish soldiers captured during the Gallipoli, or Dardanelles, campaign, which cost about half a million lives.

Gallipoli. The fighting there resulted in an enormous number of deaths—205,000 British, 47,000 French, and 250,000 Turkish. In 1917, Russia withdrew from the war because of its own internal revolution and an economy in ruins. Even without Russia, however, the Allied forces were much too great for the Central Powers. In the fall of 1918, World War I ended. Although the Allies were victorious, the price paid in human lives was great—the total number of deaths reached more than seventeen million. With the Ottomans' full surrender, the Allies occupied all strategic locations in Turkey, including the imperial city of Istanbul. The British remained a force in the former Ottoman capital until 1923.

The Allies then divided up the Ottoman Empire. Greece was given western Anatolia. The Armenians established their first republic in 1918. In 1919, the Greeks were also in control of major cities in western Anatolia, such as Izmir and Bursa. France took control of Syria and Lebanon. Britain held control of Iraq, Palestine, and Jordan. In the Balfour Declaration, the British announced its intentions of creating a Jewish state in Palestine (the state of Israel was officially established in 1948).

Winston Churchill, who was Britain's colonial secretary, played a significant role in carving out the boundaries of Iraq "with little thought to the divergent groups now locked within the same borders," according to the Foundation for Economic Education. He merged three Ottoman provinces dominated respectively by Shiites, Sunnis, and Kurds. The maps drawn after World War I continue to influence tensions and politics in the region to this day.

THE TURKISH REPUBLIC IS BORN

In the end, Turkey would not accept being totally broken up. Mustafa Kemal Atatürk, a successful Ottoman army officer, organized a resistance to the peace settlement being imposed by the Allies. In 1920, he announced that Turkey would create its own parliament. In 1922, Atatürk and his men retook Izmir, Bursa, and Edirne from the Greeks. They also reclaimed some territories in Anatolia that were given to Armenia. That same year, the Allies agreed to a new treaty stating that Atatürk's new nationalist government was Turkey's sole representative body. A new independent Turkey was established with its current borders.

After World War I, Mustafa Kemal Atatürk founded the Republic of Turkey. He promoted Western ideals and customs, including ballroom dancing, which he is seen here doing at his daughter's wedding.

In 1922, the Ottoman dynasty was officially abolished. In 1923, the Republic of Turkey was proclaimed, and Mustafa Kemal was unanimously elected president. He transformed the Turkish government, abolishing the caliphate (the Islam-based government that had once dominated the Middle East). He separated religion from government; education also became secular (nonreligious). He believed that Turkey had to Westernize to industrialize and modernize. He banned wearing the fez, a type of hat traditionally worn in the Mediterranean, which he saw a symbol of the old Ottoman Empire, and he encouraged Western dress. Although Atatürk maintained an authoritarian rule, he established elections, gave women the right to vote, and improved literacy by opening schools and strengthening the education system.

THE OTTOMAN LEGACY

The Ottoman impact lives on in culture to this day. When you walk into a Starbucks or other coffeehouse in the world, you have the Ottomans to thank. European interest in coffee came from the Turks, who popularized the eye-opening drink and opened the first coffeehouses in early Istanbul where people would go to relax and talk. Ottomans excelled at many crafts. They were master artisans who made ornately designed carpets and ceramics. Their handiwork in weaving rugs and producing fine porcelain and pottery is still highly valued. Another lasting contribution was the deeply upholstered seat or footrest without a back known as the Ottoman. This furniture originated in Turkey in the late 1700s. While Ottomans designed magnificent temples, they also popularized the small open-air building known as the kiosk.

The Ottomans pursued an interest in science and math and are notable for work in astronomy and geography. From early times, they conducted studies in astronomy and timekeeping, which can be an important part of religious

Ottomans were known for their contributions to astronomy and geography. In 1513, Ottoman admiral Piri Reis created this detailed map of the world.

duties. In the 1500s, the Ottoman inventor Taqi al-Din built an early practical steam engine, an accurate mechanical alarm clock, and a type of telescope. Under Selim I and Süleyman the Magnificent, Ottoman geographer Muhiddin Piri, also known as Piri Reis, completed a map of the world. He recorded extensive information about navigation and nautical astronomy. The idea of vaccinations may have started in Turkey as well. Reports in the 1700s revealed that doctors in the Ottoman Empire were injecting smallpox scabs into individuals, which appeared to provide some protection from the disease.

The Ottomans made a lasting contribution to the Islamic religion, spreading it through much of western Asia and into eastern Europe. They demonstrated the effectiveness of swift, organized, and at times brutal military tactics and how to rule with both absolute authority and with tolerance for others. They also cultivated the arts and architecture, put forth laws to maintain justice, accepted other ethnicities and religions, and welcomed diversity. The empire was at its height when it demonstrated the spirit embodied in the following words of Süleyman the Magnificent:

If you want to see your subjects happy
Do not be arrogant, think that they may be
better than yourself.
We are all brothers; we must love each other
Do not hibernate; be awake on your throne
Our strong hands hold the fate of the World.
We have to fight to earn
The regard and affection of men.

TIMELINE

500s Turkish tribes are identified in Chinese texts.
570 The prophet Muhammad is born.
674 Islam is introduced to Turkish tribes in central Asia.
900s Uyghur Turks convert to Islam.
900s The powerful Oghuz tribe forms in central Asia.
1000s Seljuqs, a group of Oghuz Turks, take control of the Islamic caliphate.
1063 Alp-Arslan, the "Lion Hero," becomes leader of the Seljuq Turks.
1071 Alp-Arslan and Seljuq forces seize Manzikert in eastern Anatolia from the Byzantine Empire.
1077 Seljuqs form the Sultanate of Rum, ruling a major portion of Anatolia.
1095 Christian armies assist the Byzantines in regaining territory.
1243 The Sultanate of Rum becomes a Mongol protectorate.
1258 Osman, founder of the Ottomans, is born.
1299 Osman becomes leader of the Ottoman dynasty.
Early 1300s Osman and his men capture many Byzantine cities in northwestern Anatolia.
1326 Ottomans seize the Byzantine city of Bursa.
1326 Osman dies in Sogut.
1354 The Ottomans establish a base in Europe in Gallipoli.
1361 Sultan Murat I captures Adrianople in Europe, renames it Edirne, and makes it the capital of the Ottoman Empire.
1376 Murat forms the janissaries, an elite military unit manned by captured Christian boys.
1389 Ottomans defeat Serb forces in a major battle at Kosovo Field ("the field of blackbirds").
1393 Ottomans capture Tarnovo, the capital of Bulgaria.
1396 Sultan Beyazit defeats Christian Crusaders led by King Sigismund of Hungary.
1402 The Mongol lord Timur captures Beyazit and keeps him in a cage until his death.

TIMELINE

1422 Murat II attempts to take Constantinople and fails.
1433 Ottomans conquer northern Greece.
1451 Mehmet II becomes the sultan of the Ottoman Empire.
May 29, 1453 Constantinople falls to Mehmet II's forces. Constantinople becomes Istanbul and the new capital of the Ottoman Empire.
1517 The Ottomans acquire the lands of northern Egypt, and the holy cities of Mecca and Medina fall under their rule.
1520 The forty-six-year reign of Süleyman the Magnificent begins.
1529 The Ottoman attempt to take Vienna is thwarted.
1558 The Süleymaniye Mosque is completed.
1566 Süleyman dies, and the Ottoman Empire begins its long decline.
1683 The second attempt by Ottomans to take Vienna fails.
1683 Hungary is freed from Ottoman power.
1699 After war with Austria, Russia, Venice, and Poland, the Ottomans surrender lands in central and southeastern Europe.
1768–74 The Ottoman-Russian War is fought.
1798 Napoleon makes conquests in northern Egypt.
1853 The Ottoman Empire is called the Sick Man of Europe.
1853–56 The Crimean War is fought.
1877–78 The Russo-Turkish War is fought.
1909 The Young Turks force the sultan from power, and a constitutional monarchy is established.
1914 The Ottoman Empire sides with Central Powers in World War I.
1915 The costly battle at Gallipoli is waged. Hundreds of thousands of lives are lost on both sides.
1918 World War I ends.
1922 The Ottoman dynasty is officially abolished, bringing an end to the Ottoman Empire.
1923 The Republic of Turkey is born.

GLOSSARY

allegiance Loyalty or commitment to a superior or to a group or cause.

authoritarian Demanding that people completely obey those in positions of authority as opposed to allowing individual freedoms.

barbarian A member of one of the peoples in ancient Europe who did not belong to the Greek or Roman civilizations. Barbarians were seen as uncivilized or primitive.

caliph A spiritual leader of Islam.

caravan A group of people, especially traders or pilgrims, traveling together across a desert in Asia or north Africa.

circumvent To find a way around an obstacle.

compensate To give money or something of value in return for something (such as work) or as payment for something lost or damaged.

concubine A woman who lives with a man but has lower status than his wife or wives.

confiscate To take or seize (someone's property) with authority.

constitution A body of fundamental principles, beliefs, and laws by which a country, state, or organization is governed.

Crusade Any of the military expeditions undertaken by the Christians of Europe in the eleventh, twelfth, and thirteenth centuries for the recovery of land from the Muslims.

genocide The deliberate and systematic destruction of a racial, political, or cultural group.

hierarchy A system or organization in which people or groups are ranked one above the other according to status or authority.

legacy Something handed down from the past, as from an ancestor or predecessor. It is often something for which a person wants to be remembered.

medrese Turkish term referring to school or college, usually for the study of the Islamic religion. In Arabic, the word is madrasa.

mosque A Muslim house of worship.
multiculturalism A view that the various cultures in a society deserve equal respect; a coexistence of diverse cultures.
nomad A member of a people who do not reside in a permanent location but travel from place to place to live.
parliament A representative body having supreme legislative powers within a state or organization.
principality A small territory that is ruled by a prince.
prophecy A divinely inspired prediction from a prophet.
shamanism A religion that holds that non-human entities—such as animals, plants, and inanimate objects—possess a spiritual essence. The spirits can only be influenced and accessed by shamans, people who act as connections between the natural and supernatural worlds.
subordinate Under the authority or control of another within an organization or society.
sultan A political and military ruler of a Muslim country, especially of the former Ottoman Empire.
sultanate A state or country governed by a sultan.

FOR MORE INFORMATION

The Aga Khan Museum
77 Wynford Drive
Toronto, ON M3C 1K1
Canada
(416) 646-4665
Website: https://www.agakhanmuseum.org
The Aga Khan Museum features art and artifacts from across the Muslim world, from the eighth through the twenty-first centuries. Visitors can also view manuscripts or watch films and live events hosted by the museum.

American Friends of Turkey
1025 Connecticut Avenue NW, Suite 1000
Washington, DC 20036
(202) 327-5450
Website: http://www.americanfriendsofturkey.org/
This charitable organization has programs and activities that promote greater public awareness and understanding of Turkey's history, culture, and modern-day society.

American Turkish Society
54 West 40th Street
New York, NY 10018
(646) 434-4409
Website: http://www.americanturkishsociety.org/
The oldest American-Turkish organization shares the history, culture, and art of Turkey. It also promotes tourism and serves the Turkish community in America.

Anatolian Artisans
11325 Empire Lane
North Bethesda, MD 20852
(301) 231-8128
Website: http://www.anatolianartisans.org

This group focuses on raising awareness about arts and culture in Turkey. It organizes exhibitions, festivals, fairs, conferences, and seminars.

Council of Turkish Canadians
2706 Alta Vista Drive, Suite 801
Ottawa, ON K1V 7T4
Canada
(888) 478-4333
Website: http://www.turkishcanadians.com
This nonprofit organization carries out advocacy for the interests of Canadians of Turkish origin. It promotes better understanding of the Turkish heritage, history, culture, and values in Canada.

The Institute of Turkish Studies
Intercultural Center 305R
Georgetown University
Washington, DC 20057-1033
(202) 687-0292
Website: http://turkishstudies.org/
This institute supports individual scholars, especially younger members of the academic profession in the United States, for advanced research on Turkish history and culture as well as contemporary political, social, and economic developments in Turkey.

WEBSITES

Because of the changing nature of Internet links, Rosen Publishing has developed an online list of websites related to the subject of this book. This site is updated regularly. Please use this link to access this list:
http://www.rosenlinks.com/RFE/otto

FOR FURTHER READING

Aksakal, Mustafa. *The Ottoman Road to War in 1914: The Ottoman Empire and the First World War*. New York, NY: Cambridge University Press, 2010.

Anderson, Scott. *Lawrence in Arabia: War, Deceit, Imperial Folly and the Making of the Modern Middle East*. New York, NY: Anchor, 2014.

Angold, Michael. *The Fall of Constantinople to the Ottomans: Context and Consequences*. Oxford, England: Taylor & Francis, 2014.

Casale, Giancarlo. *The Ottoman Age of Exploration*. New York, NY: Oxford University Press, 2010.

Clot, Andre. *Suleiman the Magnificent*. London, England: Saqi Books, 2012.

Deans, William. *History of the Ottoman Empire: From the Earliest Period to the Present Time*. London, England: Forgotten Books, 2015.

Donaldson, Madeleine. *Turkey* (Country Explorers). Minneapols, MN: Lerner Classroom, 2011.

Finkel, Caroline. *Osman's Dream: The History of the Ottoman Empire*. New York, NY: Basic Books, 2007.

Freely, John. *The Grand Turk: Sultan Mehmet II—Conqueror of Constantinople and Master of an Empire*. New York, NY: The Overlook Press, 2009.

Imber, Colin. *The Ottoman Empire, 1300–1650: The Structure of Power*. New York, NY: Palgrave Macmillan, 2009.

Isom-Verhaaren, Christine, and Kent F. Schull, eds. *Living in the Ottoman Realm: Empire and Identity, 13th to 20th Centuries*. Bloomington, IN: Indiana University Press, 2016.

Mathisen, Ralph W. *Ancient Mediterranean Civilizations*. Cary, NC: Oxford University Press, 2014.

For Further Reading

McKinley, Herald P. *Persia, the Rise of Islam, and the Holy Roman Empire*. New York, NY: Cavendish Square, 2015.

Palmer, Alan. *The Decline and Fall of the Ottoman Empire*. New York, NY: Fall River Press, 2011.

Rogan, Eugene. *The Fall of the Ottomans: The Great War in the Middle East*. New York, NY: Basic Books: 2015.

Ruggiero, Adriane. *The Ottoman Empire*. Tarrytown, NY: Marshall Cavendish: 2003.

Stone, Norman. *Turkey: A Short History*. London, England: Thames & Hudson, 2012.

Wheatcroft, Andrew. *The Enemy at the Gate: Habsburgs, Ottomans, and the Battle for Europe*. New York: Basic Books, 2010.

BIBLIOGRAPHY

Abiva, Huseyin, and Nora Durkee. *A History of Muslim Civilization*. Skokie, IL: IQRA´ International Educational Foundation, 2003.

Alkhateeb, Firas. "Birth of the Ottoman Empire." Lost Islamic History. January 21, 2013 (http://lostislamichistory.com/the-birth-of-the-ottoman-empire/).

Amin, Hira. "The Decline of the Ottoman Empire." MuslimMatters.org. December 20, 2011 (http://muslimmatters.org/2011/12/20/part-i-the-decline-of-the-ottoman-empire/).

Anooshahr, Ali. *The Ghazi Sultans and the Frontiers of Islam: A Comparative Study of the Late Medieval and Early Modern Periods*. New York, NY: Routledge, 2009.

Atli, Altay. "Sick Man of Europe?" Turkey in the First World War. Retrieved December 8, 2015 (http://www.turkeyswar.com/prelude/sickmanofeurope.html).

BBC. "Ottoman Empire (1301-1922)." September 4, 2009 (http://www.bbc.co.uk/religion/religions/islam/history/ottomanempire_1.shtml).

Davis, Lucile. *Life During the Great Civilizations: The Ottoman Empire*. Farmington Hills, MI: Blackbirch Press, 2004.

Freely, John. *A History of Ottoman Architecture*. Southampton, England: WIT Press, 2011.

History. "Byzantine Empire." Retrieved December 8, 2015 (http://www.history.com/topics/ancient-history/byzantine-empire).

Imber, Colin. *The Ottoman Empire*. New York, NY: Palgrave Macmillan, 2002.

Inalcik, Hanil. *An Economic and Social History of the Ottoman Empire*. New York, NY: Cambridge University Press, 1994.

Pew Research Center. "Sunni and Shia Muslims." January 27, 2011 (http://www.pewforum.org/2011/01/27/future-of-the-global-muslim-population-sunni-and-shia/).

Pittman, Paul, and Nicholas J. Pappas. *Rise of the Turks and the Ottoman Empire*. Washington, DC: Federal Research Division of the Library of Congress, 1986.

Quataert, Donald. *The Ottoman Empire, 1700-1922*. New York, NY: Cambridge University Press, 2000.

Ruggiero, Adriane. *Cultures of the Past: The Ottoman Empire*. Tarrytown, NY: Benchmark Books, 2003.

Sansal, Burak. "The Ottoman Empire." All About Turkey. Retrieved December 8, 2015 (http://www.allaboutturkey.com/ottoman.htm).

Shaw, Stanford. *The History of the Ottoman Empire and Modern Turkey: Empire of the Gazis*. New York, NY: Cambridge University Press, 1976.

United Human Rights Council. "Armenian Genocide." Retrieved December 8, 2015 (http://www.unitedhumanrights.org/genocide/armenian_genocide.htm).

Zürcher, Erik. *Turkey: A Modern History*. New York, NY: I.B. Tauris, 2007.

INDEX

ABOUT THE AUTHOR

Don Rauf is the author of more than thirty nonfiction books for young adults, including *Killer Lipstick and Other Spy Gadgets*, *American Inventions*, and *Historical Serial Killers*. He dedicates this book to his father-in-law, Fernando Vescia, who had a deep appreciation and extensive knowledge of world history.

PHOTO CREDITS

Cover, p. 1 Sufi/Shutterstock.com; p. 4 Private Collection/The Stapleton Collection/Bridgeman Images; pp. 8, 19, 42-43 DEA/G. Dagli Orti/De Agostini/Getty Images; p. 12 ZU_09/E+/Getty Images; p. 14 Izzet Keribar/Lonely Planet Images/Getty Images; pp. 16, 24, 35, 50 Heritage Images/Hulton FIne Art Collection/Getty Images; p. 21 Leemage/Universal Images Group/Getty Images; p. 26 DEA Picture Library/De Agostini/Getty Images; p. 28 Ayhan Altun/Moment/Getty Images; p. 30 Universal History Archive/Universal Images Group/Getty Images; p. 32 DEA/A. Dagli Orti/De Agostini/Getty Images; p. 33 Apic/Hulton Archive/Getty Images; p. 37 DEA/Ara Guler/De Agostini/Getty Images; p. 39 Rischgitz/Hulton Archive/Getty Images; p. 46 Interim Archives/Archive Photos/Getty Images; p. 48 Hulton Archive/Getty Images; interior pages background image © iStockphoto.com/somnuk

Designer: Brian Garvey; Editor: Shalini Saxena; Photo Researcher: Nicole Baker